GETTING THERE

Ruth Dearnley

SPRING HARVEST

Equipping the Church for action

Foreword

If you have ever taken a long car journey with small children you will know that some questions can drive you to the point of insanity.

If you have ever sat in an exam room staring in abject terror at a list of topics about which you know precious little, you will know that some questions expose your weaknesses.

If you have ever been mentored by a patient encourager, wholly committed to your growth and development, you will have discovered that some questions bring out the best in you.

In fact, those kind of questions can astonish you. Because they lead to answers.

Ruth Dearnley has put together a collection of sharp questions – and she does so in the spirit of the friendly mentor. Questions to make us think, listen, look, learn, discover and – hopefully – change.

The questions are for those who lead or take responsibility in the local church. They are designed to help us carefully consider what being church means and to push us towards asking the Lord of the Church what he thinks.

Which is the most important question of all.

Rev Ian Coffey

Spring Harvest Leadership Team and
Senior Minister, Mutley Baptist Church, Plymouth, Devon

ISBN 1 899 78843 3
Typeset by Spring Harvest and printed in the UK by Halcyon

CONTENTS

CHAPTER 1

More Questions than Answers

Introduction

Getting there eventually

What with a lack of sleep and high stress levels, I somehow managed to find myself on the wrong bus. The name of my home town was on the front. There it was in capitals. Let's face it, 'Hook' is not a word you are in danger of misreading. So, tired and emotional, I purchased my ticket. The journey was meant to be twenty minutes – on a bad day. One hour later, after a trip around surrounding suburbia, reaching parts I had never reached before, the bus stopped at a bus depot... a long way from home.

The bus driver looked round and taking compassion on this lone woman left on his bus, he asked: "You all right, love?"

My reply was quiet and to the point: "Aren't you going to Hook?"

"No," he said, with irritating certainty.

I have always prided myself that I am a calm woman. I can give the outward appearance of being in control, even if, inwardly, I am losing it. Yet this time I had no inner reserves to draw on and found myself speaking in a raised voice. The words would not read well in this context, so allow me to give you the gist.

"Why does it say Hook on the front of the bus then?"

He looked startled at the manner and content of the question.

"Does it?" he said, and we accompanied each other out of the bus and stood in the darkness staring at the dimly lit sign. There it was. Triumphant, I looked at him – the victor eyeing the conquered.

"Oh yeah, it says Hook because we go near to Hook but we don't actually go to Hook!"

I was back home an hour and a half later. I was kindly driven on my bus to the point that was as near to Hook as you could get on its return route. From there I walked.

Amazingly, I laughed out loud on the walk home as I recalled the past few hours: the bizarre nature of a sign that states a destination that you will never actually reach.

How often is the church like that?

We are a community, a people, on a journey. We identify ourselves in all sorts of ways. We are distinctive from the wider community but serve it, and have a mission to see people climb on board. We may know the direction we are supposed to be heading, but often find ourselves taking numerous detours down roads that lead us to destinations that are miles from where we should be. Whatever the distinctive features about our particular bus, the important thing is having a sense of where we have come from, what route we're taking and where we are going.

Explanations

What is this book for?

A clear aim This book has one aim – to help local congregations, and those who lead them, face the issues that most impact their future. It's for those with a deep desire to continue building a church that is strong, relevant and an honourable servant of God in the community in which they live.

A self-diagnostic approach It is based on a conviction that you are one best placed to find the answers most relevant to your situation, but finding the right answers demands asking the right questions. So here are four hundred of them – each opening an area of exploration towards the future.

A flexible resource This book can be used in a variety of ways according to your needs: for personal reflection, as a tool to help the leadership of the church, or in home groups to help the congregation reflect. It is not a 'start at the front and work through' publication. You decide the issues most relevant to your situation and plunge in at that point.

Uncertain times

The church in the United kingdom has reached a critical point in its history. There are many signs that it is alive and active. Some churches have a very active role in their communities, initiating and running projects for specific groups of people. Churches of all traditions are seeing their congregations grow in number and in faith. Many are bringing the gospel of hope to hopeless situations.

We know, however, that the church is facing an uncertain future. In other parts of the world, it is seeing continual growth – but we are not. Although there may be pockets of local church growth, the overall picture is one where we are bleeding to death – becoming smaller and more irrelevant. However long our own church has been around, we all belong to a church that has a tradition of some sort. It may involve candles, guitars, choirs or overhead projectors. It may be a rural village congregation or an eclectic cathedral or suburban community church. It may be urban or suburban. Our tradition offers us a rich tapestry to hold onto and it offers the challenge to let go of things that are now inhibiting the community from fulfilling its vision.

The society we live in has changed radically and is continually changing – both locally, nationally and internationally. As the church in the United kingdom, we need to be aware of the pressures on people, the changing moral tide, the impact of multi-culturalism – to name just a few. Most people no longer see this as a Christian country. We immerse ourselves in means of communicating that use books less and less. We are living in a country that is multi-faith, where individuals are becoming more aware of their rights and freedom of choice. To many religion is a waste of time and irrelevant and yet there is a deepening sense that all our lives and relationships are fragile, regardless of where we live or who we are.

Ask the question

What will the church's role be in society in the future? No church leader can avoid asking questions, and no church can evade the need to look at what it is achieving and where it is going. This book of questions is for anyone, in any church, who is open to fresh challenges and serious thinking about the future. We need to ask these questions – and listen to each other's answers – with no agenda other than to understand one another. That way we will make the right decisions, and understand why we did so.

How to use the book

There are about four hundred questions in the book. They are divided into four main chapters with the titles:

Within each chapter the material covers specific aspects of the life of a church. Each chapter is divided into different sections, and each of these focuses on a different aspect of church life. Use the contents list to select the section you want. But be warned – if you choose to work through the whole book at once, the sheer volume and range of questions could overwhelm you. Decide what key issues face your church at the moment – go to the appropriate questions and use them as a starting point to thinking and discussion.

With a more long-term view the material can be used to:

▶ Assess a church's strengths, resources and gifts.
▶ Help a church to perceive what its role is now within the local community, what it can be and what it should be.
▶ Work alongside initiatives that your church is already planning.
▶ Offer important questions to help leaders assess the church they serve, or to assess a church they are thinking of serving.
▶ Help a church council, PCC, area meetings (e.g. deanery or circuit or cluster) or other group to spark discussion and follow emerging ideas appropriate to a wider geographical area.
▶ Provide the congregation in home groups or cell groups with a way to be involved.

Information Points

At the end of each group of questions there is an information point. This is a list of resources to follow up that subject. It will complement the ones you know already and suggest others.

You've got mail

At the beginning of each chapter the blue section introduces the churches John wrote to in Revelation: Sardis, Laodicea, Ephesus, Pergamum, Thyatira, Smyrna and Philadelphia. There is a brief overview of what was happening in those churches when they got mail, and what was happening in the cities in which they were based. What pressures were the churches facing? What were their strengths and needs?

For resources to do a deeper study of these letters and the churches they were sent to, go to the relevant information point

An Uncertain Future

Facing an uncertain future is not unique to us. This was the experience of the seven churches described in Revelation 1-3. Two of the churches were in grave danger, three were neither very good nor very bad, and two were in good shape. However, the trend was towards decline.

The first century was drawing to a close and for those early believers, it was a time of turbulence and in some cases oppression. Nero had begun his persecution of the Christians twenty five years earlier and now the Emperor Domitian was in charge. His antagonism was beginning to be felt in Asia Minor. The Apostle John was in exile on the Isle of Patmos, forty miles off the coast. From there he wrote to meet the needs of the churches. Their letters were meant to be shared with the other churches, so all could benefit.

> *i* **Information Point**
> *Spring Harvest Study Guide 2002*
> *You've got mail*, Stephen Travis: Spring Harvest Publishing 2002
> *What Christ thinks of the church*, John Stott: Spring Harvest/Candle Books 2002
> *The Book of Revelation*, G K Beake - New International Greek Testament
>   commentary - Eerdmans Paternoster 1999
> *Revelation, Tyndale New Testament Commentary*, Leon Morris

We've got mail

Revelation 1:1 begins 'The revelation of Jesus Christ...' Revelation is about Christ, his might and power. The seven churches, under pressure, didn't need a puzzle book or a conundrum to occupy their mind but a fresh vision of the risen Jesus. Now we read the letters to the churches and find that they contain warnings, challenges and encouragement for us. We've got mail too. It causes us to ask questions of ourselves. The replies may not be what we want to hear, but if we have the strength and will to ask the right questions at the right times we will discern and discover what we think and what we want to do

The Church as community

The church, wherever it is, whoever is a part of it and whatever it does, is a community. Not just named by buildings or geography - although they contribute to its identity - the church is a group of people. It is all ages, with diverse views and needs, and where people are part of the church community in very different ways. Yet together we are the community of Christ in that place.

This book looks at the following issues:

Chapter 2 – The Church – a living Community
Background to Sardis (Rev. 3:1-6) and Laodicea (Rev. 3:14-22)

How do we love our community? What does that mean? Love is a much-maligned word or can often lack integrity when put into action. What does that lead us to see and then do? What have love and servant hood got in common? Discuss the priorities – to love or to believe – about issues of ethics and its repercussions for leadership.

Chapter 3 – The Church – a loving community
Background to Ephesus (Rev.2:1-7)

How do we live in our community? These are the communities we know about that we contribute to and that give to us. What does our community mean to us and how do we recognise it? For those of us who spend most of the week somewhere different to where we live what impact does that have on how we define our community. What are the ecumenical issues we have to face. What have been the fruits and the challenges working in this area?

Chapter 4 – The Church – a loyal community
Background to Pergamum (Rev.2:12-17) and Thyatira (Rev.2:18-29)

How can we be loyal to the faith that we are called to live? What is our attitude to the truth? How do we view loyalty? There has to be an element of journey in this section as it will relate to how people's faith has developed and been encouraged to grow and what that means in respect to their view of faith and what it is that they have developed a loyalty to. How is our doctrine expressed in our worship?

Chapter 5 – The Church – a long suffering community
Back ground to Smyrna (Rev.2:8-11) and Philadelphia (Rev.3:7-13)

To a community that suffers what do we offer? – what sort of people are we in the face of suffering? This directly affects how we view the suffering of our community. What do we see as suffering or the needs of our community and how can the church address this effectively? What are the long-term connections with our communities? How have they grown in recent years? We will look at the relationship of faith /church schools and the long term role they can play? How does the church view youth work and how they are an active part of the church? We need to see into the distance where we are taking them and where they are taking us.

The Church as a living community

The churches of Sardis and Laodicea

To the church at Sardis, Jesus says 'I know what you are doing. People say you are alive but in fact you are dead.'

To the church in Laodicea, He says 'I know what you are doing but you are neither hot nor cold.'

Both these churches had a tendency towards spiritual sleep or death. Christ is revealed to them as the awesome victor of life. He is the active living God and without him we drift into the sleep or death. The Nicene creed declares He is the Lord, the giver of life. The churches at Sardis and Laodicea had seen better days – just like the cities in which they made their home.

Sardis was a city with an illustrious past. An earthquake had devastated Sardis eighty years before John's letter was written. It had been rebuilt with Roman money but never quite recovered. Its greatness lived on in the folklore and memories of the people. It was living in the powerful deception of past reputation – and so was the church. The people of the city were so convinced of their own safety, they didn't even bother to post watches in time of war – until Cyrus' men scaled the cliff face in the darkness in 546BC. This seemingly impregnable city had twice fallen to surprise attacks.

William Barclay wrote:

> *'Sardis was a city of peace, not the peace won through battle, but the peace of the man whose dreams are dead and whose mind is asleep, the peace of lethargy and evasion.'*
>
> **William Barclay – Letters to the Seven Churches.**

John Stott wrote:

> *'Its reputation as a progressive church had evidently spread far and wide ... it was known by the other six churches in the province for its vitality. "What a live church you have in Sardis!" visitors would exclaim with admiration. ... and so no doubt it appeared. Its congregation was probably large for those days with money resources and excellent projects. There was every indication of life and vigour but this socially distinguished congregation was a spiritual graveyard. ... it had a name for virility and no right to its name.'*

Laodicea was a banking and judicial centre and had a thriving textile industry. It also had a medical school, which specialised in ophthalmology. In AD60, it too was destroyed by an earthquake but the city had rebuilt itself from its own resources, declining help from Rome. The inhabitants prided themselves on being dependent on no one. The city and the church had a good reputation but this could not be relied upon for the future. The city of Laodicea had a particular challenge because of its lack of a hot and cold water supply. They had to suffer lukewarm water and Jesus calls them away from lukewarm faith.

Both churches had come from an uncertain background. There is sparse evidence of how they came to be founded. With Sardis and Laodicea, there is no good news preface yet a loving wake up call. They were complacent and not watchful – the sleeping churches.

> 'Like a chameleon, the church at Sardis and Laodicea simply melted into its surroundings and became indistinguishable from them. It had become outstandingly successful in the art of camouflage.'

Stephen Travis

What is the purpose of church?

These first four questions drive us to look and ask about our true identity and purpose. They are part of the work we have to do but are best done alongside the more accessible questions about the practicalities of our churches and the way they work.

◗ **What is church?**
How can we address this, taking into account our history but also looking at the present and the future with realistic eyes?

◗ **What is the church for?**
Is it to bring the kingdom or be the kingdom or act out the kingdom?

◗ **Who is the church?**
What are the differences between the church and the kingdom?

◗ **Who is the church for?**
Is it for the elect few or is it to be the servant of God for all those who live in a particular community?

What is the purpose of the local church?

The churches at Sardis and Laodicea had fallen asleep. Let's stand back and look at our church. What is its purpose? We will then begin to see what sleeping sickness looks like.

(Warning – it is easy to jump to simplistic conclusions. We may decide that an old building, an ageing congregation, quiet services and a traditional format mean a church that is sleeping, whereas a large congregation packed with young people and full of exciting projects means a wide-awake church. We may be wrong.)

Select your top five in order of priority and then to discuss what it would be that would indicate it was in danger of falling asleep.

Is the church to be a presence in the community?
▶ a place that offers answers?
▶ a place of friendships?
▶ a place where the good news is shared?
▶ a place where the truth is proclaimed?
▶ a safe place?
▶ a place that is constant in an ever changing world?
▶ a place which is on the move and never stands still?
▶ a place where the people have vision?
▶ a place where you can find or meet with God?

The history/reputation of your church

What do you know about the history of your church?
▶ What's informed the journey of your church so far, since you have been in the church and before you arrived?
▶ Do you know enough about how the church has been influenced by people in the past – leaders, structures etc – and if not, how would you find out relevant and helpful information?
▶ Particularly as a church leader, what is the broad vision and good understanding of the past as well as the future? What has been the long-term work achieved under different past leaders? What different gifts did they have?
▶ Has the church any uncharted water? What are the aspects of church life that have not been given priority in the last five years that need attention? What are the areas or issues that have never been raised that need raising?
▶ Is the way ahead clear, urgent, or complex and what makes it so? Why and what does that mean for the leadership?

- What are the unresolved issues, which are stopping the church moving forward?
- How are they to be addressed – or can they be?

Honest reflection

Are we getting there?
Looking from the perspective of someone within the church:
- How has their own vision for their church become weary or single focused?
- What are your dreams for the future. (This is not an opportunity for everyone to say why they think their church is great or not!)

Looking at it from the perspective of someone outside of the church community:
- How much does the church connect with the wider local community? Is it a sleeping animal that occasionally prowls around after money, or stages the odd big event?

All of the following are elements of church life. Which are the ones that are present in your church? How could you find consensus of opinion from the congregation if asked which ones they thought were vital or the ones they thought were present? Put them in order of importance for a church that is getting there.
- singing songs or good hymns?
- the quality of the relationships?
- work in the community?
- good community relationships?
- openness to change?
- the amount/quality of resources/facilities available?
- committed financial giving?
- the willingness to serve in the church?
- a large and diverse staff team?
- the number of weekly meetings?
- activities for all ages?
- a structured teaching programme for all ages?
- evidence that it is `God centred'? How can you assess this?
- a genuine concern for each other?
- the inclusiveness of the community?
- a comfortable place to be in?
- a place to find and experience forgiveness?
- a place that equips its members for their lives during the rest of the week?
- a place for private faith and belief?
- a centre for the Christian family?
- a centre for the community?

Are there issues that are not here but you consider vital signs of your church life?

Reputations
What reputation does your church have?

Answer this question in relation to the following groups of local people:
▶ parents at the school gate
▶ shop owners
▶ businesses
▶ local residents
▶ other community providers

Ask these groups and find out if what you thought was true is what they really think.

Handling Change (part 1)

Initiating change:
▶ Should it be an open or closed procedure?
▶ What are the practical and psychological benefits of both?

All change, however small, will involve an element of risk.
▶ How does your church calculate such risk in considering new initiatives? These risks could be financial or other.
▶ What steps are being taken at the moment that involve an element of risk?
▶ Why is this the right time to initiate such a change?
▶ What effective indicators govern the pace of change now?
▶ How is the congregation involved throughout the process?
▶ What opportunities could be given to allow people to be heard and feel they have been heard?
▶ What do people do if they feel they are voiceless?

Having a plan
▶ What sort of plan is in place?
▶ Is it an adventurous plan or a safe meticulous one?
▶ Are there a number of short-term planned developments or a continuous long-term one?
▶ What is the intention of any short or long term change?
▶ How are the plans being communicated to the congregation and how are they being involved in the process?

Consultation process

- How is the consultation process going to move change forward?
- Is the process for change proving successful or does it need adjusting?
- Is there confusion about what's going on?
- Is there a need for a change in approach?
- Is the opposition growing or being won over?
- Is there confusion over the facts? Who is confused? Is this expected or unusual? So what next?
- Who is coping with the fall-out?

Completion

- What will completion of this change look like?
- How will it be marked?
- When it is completed, what will the congregation have learnt about the process of change for next time?

Leadership issues when handling change

- There are always those threatening to leave unless this or that changes..... and those who will leave if you change this or that....how does the church handle this?
- What strategies and structures are in place to help you as leader/s cope with this tension?
- When is it right for the leadership to say what they really think?
- When, if at all, is it right for the leader to take action despite opposition or the lack of a strong consensus of support?
- For a member of the congregation or church community that wants something to change how do you best communicate that within the existing structures?

Information Point

Ministry Issues: mapping the trends Gordon Kuhrt – Church House Publishing (CHP)

Building Missionary Congregations Robert Warren (CHP)

Details of Church House Publishing books can be obtained from:
Church House Publishing
31 Great Smith Street
London SW1P 3BN
t.   0207 898 1306
e.   publishing@c-of-e.org.uk

Handling Conflict

This is usually linked with change but it does not have to be.

▶ What are the most common arguments and tensions that exist within the congregation?

▶ How long have they been there?

▶ How are these being addressed?

▶ How will these tensions be resolved?

▶ Has the church moved on over a given period of time?

> **ℹ Information Point**
> *A Church Shaped for Mission* (CHP/Methodist Publishing House)

Supporting networks for leadership

▶ What are the supporting structures within the church community for leaders?

▶ Are there ecumenical support teams/cluster groups?

▶ What are their needs? How can a congregation be informed of leadership needs and then help?

▶ What can the church do to create a more supportive structure for the leaders?

▶ If there is an internal issue that needs mediating, who can or do the church leadership turn to?

▶ What if the leadership is divided? Are any issues where this has not been resolved?

▶ In what ways can resolution be found? Refer to past experiences where this has happened and been handled well.

▶ Whom are the leaders accountable to?

Don't just be busy – be fruitful

A living community

▶ What is fruit? (e.g. souls saved or people helped or increasing numbers or more giving!)

▶ What is the church good at doing?

▶ What activities are successful and how can the church assess this?

▶ Do you have to be able to see the outcome to assess if a particular activity is fruitful? Can we always assess this?

Assessment

▶ What long-term benefits are there in the quiet visiting, listening and building of relationships?

- What importance is given to visiting people and being available to others e.g. funeral visits or sick visiting? How could this be developed?
- Are there some things that we know are right to do, with no numerical, financial or outward signs of success for us to see? What are they?
- How does the church measure short-term results and – more importantly – long-term fruit?
- When has an activity fulfilled its purpose?

Decisions
- What's the best next step? – Is it right to stop some activities or to have a fallow period for an activity to allow review?
- Are you brave enough to stop something because everybody's tired of doing it, if it's still successful?
- Are you still slogging away at something because it once had a focus?
- Is the leadership changing things too quickly in order to move on, and leaving a proportion of the people behind – creating a divided congregation?

Using people's gifts

- What gifts are there in the congregation that are not being used?
- In the leadership, who is intuitive and can see those who need to be urged to think about the next step and use the gifts they have?
- How are they approached?
- Are they given enough space to respond? It is true that you may train people and then they move – so other churches benefit from that training – we can see this as equipping the wider church.
- Is there an expectancy to serve and not just visit and watch –and is the balance right between expectancy and pressure?
- How does the staff team spot gifts and encourage people to use them?
- How key is the encouragement given to those who accept the invitation and what continuing support is there?

Don't be squeezed into a mould

This refers to Sardis and Laodicea and the influence the surrounding culture has on the church community.

Squeezing by church tradition
- How do we maintain our tradition and connect with our culture? This question is a

not easy and challenges all of us to stand aside and look at our tradition. It makes no difference whether we are Anglican, Brethren, New Frontiers, Baptist, Salvation Army, Methodist, Pioneer, Catholic, United Reformed, FIEC, Pentecostal, Ichthus, Church of Scotland, Church of Wales or any other independent church network.

▶ What are the strengths of our tradition?
▶ What are the challenges that face your tradition?
▶ Perhaps the church has always had a reputation that is now being challenged? It could be that the church has never worked with other churches in the area and there is now a wish to do that.

Squeezing by the wider community
What pressures from the wider community have affected the church life?

▶ the pressure for time on a Sunday with competing youth or adult activities
▶ the potential local drug problem that has meant shutting the church building for fear of theft – making the church less available and accessible
▶ the lack of parking space and traffic problems that means use of the church centre is limited in weekdays
▶ untrue, negative local newspaper reports which have resulted in deeper suspicion of the church and its activities

How have these been handled so far and with what success?

Has the local community squeezed the church into a mould and given it an unhelpful image?

The needs of the local community

Pressing Community Issues
▶ What are the pressing issues or challenges in the wider community and how can the church be involved?
▶ Has the role of the church in the wider community changed at all in the last few years?
▶ Is it a role that has been growing and changing?
▶ Where is it heading?
▶ What is the next step?

Dealing with a multi-faith community
▶ How is the wider community dealing with the multi-faith issues and the effects of the wider international developments? What role can the church play in this?
▶ If such issues have a daily effect on the life of the church and the local community,

what support or guidance do the members and leadership receive?

- There is a need for every church, in whatever community, to address the multi-faith issue now. Different churches will act in different ways depending on their situation.
- How is the church able to work effectively with other faiths in the community?
- When and how can the church remain distinctive in its Christian identity?
- Who is key to enabling this to happen?
- What resources have you got to enable progress to be made?

i **Information Point**
Paul Blackham, All Souls Langham Place, London

Ecumenical Relationships

- Describe the relationship of your church with the other churches in the community.
- What is said by the church, if anything, about the churches in the area?
- Is what is said constructive?
- If not, why? What is the history?
- What developments have happened in the last three to five years?
- How has this benefited the local community and the local church.
- How can any suspicion and ignorance about each other be replaced by trust and openness between the local churches?
- Are the churches duplicating what they do? Is this fulfilling a need or is there a place for joining forces in particular activities?
- How are the churches distinct?
- In what ways are the churches unified?
- If there is no willingness by others to work together, what approach should your church take?

i **Information Point**
World Council of Churches

Releasing Energy – Flora Winfield (CHP)

Closure – the issue of shutting a church

Assessment

- What are the signs of a church that has lost vital signs of life?
- What can be done to help such a church?
- Is this ever an issue that has come up in the history or at present about your local church?

- What is being done about it?
- What about the possibility of new life with fresh leadership?
- What can church area re-organisation do to contribute to a solution? e.g. establishing a team or group of churches, pooling resources within an area etc.

Closure
- When is it right – if at all – to close a church?
- What are the over-riding factors that will determine the decision?
- Finances?
- Membership?
- What is the church's contribution to its own membership and the local community?
- Has it potential to change?
- Is the lack of available leaders proving insurmountable?
- Is it possible to find new leaders?

It is very painful to take the decision to close a church, but with the help of supportive church networks, it can and at times has to be done. There is also a climate of change, with church organisations having to make strategic financial decisions as part of long term plans.

CHAPTER 2

The Church – a loving community

Revelation 2 brings us the letter to the church at Ephesus. Although Pergamum was the official capital city of the province of Asia, Ephesus was by far its greatest city. All roads literally led to Ephesus. The city boasted fabulous architecture, impressive roadways, a disproportionately large population and the most important harbour in the province. It was a 'free' (self-governing) city, so no Roman soldiers were garrisoned there. It had an amazing sports stadium, the stunning Temple of Diana (one of the seven wonders of the world), and a statue of the Emperor, four times life-size depicting him as Zeus, ruler of all the gods. It had an academic pedigree with an enormous library and a religious economy. Silversmiths made an excellent living from the worship of Diana. It was home to thousands of priests and priestesses many of whom were sacred prostitutes, and served as an asylum for fleeing criminals, who contributed to the city's crime and morality problems.

The church was probably founded by Aquilla and Priscilla and strengthened by the extensive ministry of Paul. Timothy was placed in charge of the church when Paul left, and thus Timothy was called the first Bishop. The church had to live with occultism, promiscuity, a belief that life was cheap and the prevalent notion that a distant government held sway over the lives of the city's people.

The letter is a word of encouragement to answer their questions: 'Does the emperor rule?', 'No, Christ rules', 'Have we been deserted?', 'No, Christ knows what you are suffering and you are held tight in his hand.' The letter said 'Well done' – it contained praise for the work achieved and the daily battle that the church had committed itself to. Their suffering had made them constantly vigilant over the details of doctrine and in holding fast to the truth, perhaps they lost the ability to love first and last.

John was the Bishop of Ephesus for many years, and the church seemed to emulate his two best known character traits – great tenderness and the ability to act as a 'son of thunder', when love would be eclipsed by hot anger.

The two sides of John are seen again in two stories that have been handed down concerning his later years in Ephesus: he refused to stay under the same roof as the heretic Cerinthus, and he reduced all his teaching to a sermon of one sentence, which in old age he used to repeat at each meeting: `Little children, love one another.' We can tell from Acts and Ephesians that the early church was characterised by both love and zeal especially in the value she placed on sound doctrine. But in her keenness for the truth the church in Ephesus had lost its first love – the one quality without which all others are worthless.

Based on material from The Message of Revelation *Michael Wilcock BST*

The Ephesians had set out to contend for the truth only to discover that in the course of the battle they had lost the one quality without which all others are worthless. Where love for other people is lost, love for God turns into religious formalism or fanaticism.

Stephen Travis

Encouragement

What causes love and tolerance to grow in a church?
- persuasion?
- teaching it?
- people being loved?
- Who are the encouragers in the church community and what role do they play?
- How can people be encouraged in their work in the church and in their daily Christian life?

Loving one another

Discuss the obvious and less obvious ways that people are loved within the church congregation.
- How do the congregation help each other?
- Is the help they offer all words and nothing practical?
- Do people listen or is there a tendency to always have the right answers?
- Do they help or is there a tendency to always point to someone else?
- How secure are the members that they are loved by God?
- Has the church a tradition that says God is Love or God is Love if you play by our rules, if you learn our way of behaviour, if you stay around and earn your place?

Sometimes we can have hidden agendas, linked to what is preached. God's love is then offered conditionally – with the inference that people's behaviour may cause it to be withdrawn. A challenge for the church is that ultimately we should have such confidence in God's love that we can welcome and truly love others as they really are.

▶ If we believe this, how does that impact your local church?

Pastoral Care

For the church congregation:
▶ Describe the pastoral network that operates in your church community.
▶ What are its strengths?
▶ Are there situations when people's needs go unnoticed? If so, what are the reasons for this?
▶ How can the network already in place be adapted to cope with these situations?
▶ What networks or creative ways have the church got to facilitate this to happen? e.g. prayer board – prayer chain

For the wider local community:
▶ How does the church cater for the pastoral needs of the local community?
▶ What can be done to increase the pastoral care of the wider community? e.g. neighbourhood links – bereavement groups – children's groups – parenting courses – holiday schemes – homeless projects – visiting the elderly – counselling services– etc. There are many links here into mission into the community (chapter 2) and the suffering community (chapter 5).

Those who care:
▶ How is the burden of the pastoral care shared out?
▶ In the event of a pastoral need that leaves the members involved out of their depth, where does the church go for active and further assistance?
▶ Who is presently involved and how can this team expand?
▶ What factors are important to the church in selecting those who take responsibility in this area?
▶ What structures are in place that offer continuing training for those involved in this area?
▶ How can the teaching in the church about responsibility to care be enhanced and support those who take this role in the church?

The Welcome

What is your church's welcome like?
- Is there a comfortable welcome – do people want to come back?
- What greets them?
- Is the door shut?
- Who greets them?
- Is the literature, if any, attractive and readable?
- Is there a balance struck between someone being overwhelmed or being ignored?
- Have you compared your thoughts on the warmth of the church's welcome with any newcomers? What about those who have been in the church for a while, who may feel that newcomers get a warmer welcome than established members.

Catering for all:
- Are children made to feel welcome?
- What help is there if newcomers are on their own?
- What help is there for the elderly?
- What help is there for those who have not gone to a church before?

A time for opportunity and feedback:
- What do people say as they leave?
- Do people have an opportunity to talk to someone?
- What are their leaving comments?
- How can any future connection be made or organised as they leave?
- What are the hidden or subtle messages that come across? An unconditional welcome?

Service material:
- How is what happens during worship made accessible to newcomers?
- What more could be done?
- Is the service meaningful and enjoyable to those who are new and those who have been there a long time? Is this seen as achievable or not by the church?
- How has the service material changed over the last two years?
- What were the main causes of that change?
- Have any of these changes caused difficulties and if so, how are they being resolved?

_i_ **Information Point**
Liturgy Pastoral and parochial Michael Perham – SPCK, Holy Trinity Church,
Marylebone Road, London

Come and Join the Celebration

Introduction to Christian Ministry: Gordon Kuhrt (CHP)

Producing Your own Orders of Service: Mark Earey (CHP/Praxis)

Financial matters

This is a crucial factor in the life of a church. However big or small, independent or part
of a larger church network, all churches require money to spend and give away.

This is a vital sign of a growing and loving church – for a church to grow in its work
and mission, it has to financially healthy..To live in love means being able to give
financially.

Being taught to give:
▶ How is giving taught in the church?
▶ How are people educated in giving?
▶ How does the church prioritise its spending?
▶ Does the responsibility for financial matters rest on a team of people or on one
individual?
▶ What is the state of the finances?
▶ How is the church informed of the financial situation?
▶ How is the church involved in the financial matters?
▶ What is the church's attitude to financial matters?

What to spend money on:
▶ Is there a history of spending or saving or both?
▶ What have large amounts of money been spent on over the past year?
▶ Does this give any indication of how selection for spending takes place?
▶ Is there a view that it is safer to spend on the building needs rather than on training
people?
▶ Has this had a long-term impact on the church and what has it been?

Review of spending:
▶ Has there been extravagant giving with little assessment of the worthiness of the
results?

- How can necessary spending continue if the church is facing a financial shortfall?
- What networks of support are available for the treasurer/s if there are financial difficulties?

> **Information Point**
> *First to the Lord* (CHP)

Education matters

Part of the process of a church growing in love is to learn what the Christian life is about.

Who is teaching?
- What are the benefits of having a team who can teach?
- Who is doing it?
- Who else in the congregation can teach?
- How do you assess someone's potential to teach and move them forward in it?
- Have you a team that can preach or teach so that you cover different approaches and how do you utilise them?
- What training is available within your church or the wider church for teachers or preachers? Do those who teach have regular support and feedback amongst themselves and from the church community that will encourage them and keep them in touch with the people's needs?
- For those who have been executing that role for a long while is there any continued training or input available?

The desire to learn:
- What has the church done so far?
- Do people see the need to learn?

Ways to learn
- What are the different opportunities to learn?
- What are the ways in which the church learns?– in a group, individually or all together?
- How does the church create an atmosphere to learn, change your mind or say what you really think?
- How can you judge the success of the teaching? Although we know that all that we are and all that we learn is revealed by the work of the Holy Spirit, there should be some critique of teaching methods and learning in the community to adjust resources or approach.

The learning community

What different groups and ages have you got in your church community?
1. Those who have been within the church for a longer period of time and have had opportunities to learn and grow in the faith
2. Those who have been around for a significant period of time and yet have not had opportunity or desire to continue in the learning process.
3. Those who are new to the local church community and yet have a Christian journey that has involved teaching and growing in the faith.
4. Those who are new to the local church community and have no previous Christian experience.

Identify the main groups in your local church community and how best to prioritise the most appropriate learning approaches for the whole congregation.

> ***i*** **Information Point**
> *Alpha* – Alpha Office, Holy Trinity Brompton, Brompton Road, London SW7 1JA
> t.   0207 581 8255
> f.   0207 584 8536
>
> *The Emmaus Series*
>
> *The Y Course* – designed for those beyond the fringe of the church:
> t.   01908 364254
> e.   ycourse@premieronline.co.uk

Resources and methods

▶ What is the church using to teach with? e.g. the Anglican Lectionary, printed course material, individual's own plans. Is there a wide selection of adult and child learning resources available?
▶ If there is a sense that it is time to look at something different how will you select new material?
▶ Has your church community changed a lot in the last year/two years/five years and have you taken note of that in your teaching and learning?
▶ How many new teaching initiatives have there been in the past year? What time does it take to establish continuity for effective learning across the age ranges? It is important to keep a critical eye on all materials used because as the needs of the community change, so the methods and materials to teach need to be flexible.
▶ What is the best selection of medium for learning at the moment? e.g.. Written –

visual – audio experiential – discussion.

- What are the best methods of learning that suit the church facilities/buildings/ space?
- How can this space be adapted to facilitate other means for learning?

Children's learning

- Have you got enough people or is it the burden on the few?
- Is it easy to join the team of children's leaders? Do you have to have specified qualifications or is true willingness enough?
- Has the church got a good up-to-date child protection policy in place?
- Do the resources or material available give confidence to the new volunteers?
- Is there the possibility of teaching in teams of adults so that adults do not become isolated in the world of the children's learning and divorced from adult company?
- With the immense variety of children's work resources on offer, what does the church offers that will captivate their imaginations and their commitment across the different age ranges?
- How are effective connections made between the children and the adult members of the church?
- Are there opportunities for the children to lead the adults in worship, as distinct to children performing for adults?
- Are other personnel available that can look astutely and guide wisely, giving creative input and perhaps taking a mentoring role?
- Are there training courses run locally that could give input to the leaders and offer an alternative to the training and guidance available within your own local congregation?

All age learning

- What parts of your learning are appropriate for all ages?
- What does the church do well for different age groups?
- What scope is there for experimenting with times together or apart? e.g. learning new songs workshop which is an all age activity, or a young people's post confirmation cell group or family teaching morning on a combined theme instead of the morning service.

Information Point

SU resources – Scripture Union 01908 856000

CPAS; Church Pastoral Aid Society, Athena Drive, Tachbrook Park, Warwick CV34
6NG 01926 458400 www.cpas.org.uk

Video – *Veggie tales*, Big Idea Productions Inc, Word Entertainment Ltd, Milton
Keynes Bucks 01908 648440

Come to the feast, Stuart Thomas – books 1 and 2, Kevin Mayhew Ltd, Buxhall,
Stowmarket, Suffolk IP14 3BW Tel: 01449 737978 fax 01449 737834
email sales@kevinmayhewltd.com www.kevinmayhew.com

Living Stones, Susan Sayers – also available from Kevin Mayhew Ltd

Roots (Resources for all-age worship) rootsontheweb.com – The Salvation
Army Youth Division and annual conference – Director Russell Rook

Handling change (part 2)

A loving community

Part 1 (Page 15) focused on initiating change but often circumstances force change
that a church community has to deal with.

▶ What is changing at the moment due to circumstances?

▶ Are people struggling with a loss of a leader – of a church member – of focus – of
unity – of a project? Does this involve grieving?

▶ How can it be seen to be a change that brings opportunity?

▶ If the change is the arrival of new leadership with new ideas what is necessary to
make this a positive change for the church?

▶ Perhaps the church community have moved to a new site, have altered or are
planning to alter their buildings. What effect is it that having?

Information Point

Repitching the Tent – Richard Giles. The Canterbury Press, St Mary's Works,
St Mary's Plain, Norwich, Norfolk NR 3 3BH

Widening the Eye of the Needle (CCC/CHP)

How do we see our communities?

▶ What is your church's view of the local community?

▶ Is it a place to be separate from – or a place to be immersed in?

▶ Is it a place to serve? To convert?

▶ Who are the church's friends?

These are crucial questions that determine how we as church live in our communities and how the local community will view us.

▶ In what ways are we a part of our communities?
▶ How are we distinct?
▶ Are all these things helpful?
▶ How can we, as the Christian church, support one another in the difficult moments when we need to be distinct or speak out in to our local community?
▶ Where can the local church go to for advice on dealing with the local media?
▶ How does the church find a voice that is relevant in the community?
▶ What are the present strengths that the local church has in place when wanting to speak out into the community?
▶ Are there issues of justice in the local community that the church needs to get involved in?

> ### *i* **Information Point**
> *Faithworks*
>   Oasis Trust,
>   115 Southwark Bridge Road,
>   London SE1 0AX
>   t.   0207 450 9049
> *Resources for dealing with the media*: the main denominations will have their own media offices. For smaller networks or independent churches, the EA has a media office which can offer advice. 0207 207 2100
> *Good News People* by Robert Warren: Board of Mission (CHP)

Mission not maintenance

▶ What is the main understanding of mission?
▶ What events or continuing activity has the church done over the past 2-5 years that has been part of the work of mission?
▶ What works best for the church in mission?
▶ Personal, pastoral contacts
▶ Good relevant worship
▶ Wide range of organisations
▶ Preaching and teaching
▶ Other
▶ How do we best serve the community we live and work in?
▶ What has actually been done in the community in the last year?
▶ Does the church has an outreach, evangelism or mission programme?
▶ How is that being worked out in practice? Who is or could be involved?

- Is what is in place useful and appropriate?
- How would you organise a review?
- Does your church's mission extend overseas?
- What relationship is there between the pastoral role of the church in the local community and its mission?
- Are they identical?
- If not, what is the distinctiveness of mission?
- Does image matter in mission?
- How does your church's image help in its mission and what could be done to improve it?
- What effective ways does the church have for communicating to the wider community?
- How can these be improved?
- What connections and relationships are there that can facilitate the church becoming better known and well used by in the community?

Information Point

Faithworks – see above
Rebuild – see above
Launching a mission congregation – Robert Warren,
  CPAS,
  Tachbrook Park,
  Warwick CV34 6NG.
Diocesan Initiatives
Willow Creek resources

CHAPTER 3

CHAPTER 4

The church as a loyal community

Pergamum

Pergamum was a city proud of its history. It was a seat of learning with a fabulous library that held over 200,000 books, a busy medical school and a love of writing. One writer described Pergamum as being 'like a royal city, the home of authority'. It had become part of the Roman Empire not by unwilling conquest and compulsion but by spontaneous choice. So when John wrote his letter, Pergamum had been a capital for more than three hundred years. But beneath the scholarly exterior, there was something more sinister. One Christian, Antipas, had already been executed publicly.

The city was particularly famous as the headquarters for the worship of Asklepios, 'the saviour god' who was renowned for healing. The altar to Zeus was very prominent, standing on a ledge jutting our from the hillside, eight hundred feet above the city. There had been a blatant challenge to the church to back off from its loyalty to Christ, during a season that Christ describes as 'the days of Antipas'. Christ commends them for their faithfulness during this time of testing. But now they faced more subtle challenges – this time from false teachers. The Christian community at Pergamum that had done so well when confronted with outright opposition was now losing its grip on the truth, allowing erroneous doctrine to be openly spread by false teachers. The words of the letter call them to repent and be loyal to the truth.

Thyatira

Thirty-five miles down the road in the market city of Thyatira, the church had been doing well. They were commended for their work, their love and faith, their perseverance and they were maturing in faith: unlike the Ephesians, who had fallen from a former height (Rev.2:5). Now they were doing more 'than they did at first.' Lydia came from this area. Some have suggested that the church was planted from Ephesus. It was probably quite small.

Here, too, there was a danger. In Pergamum, Christians were in danger of persecution. In Thyatira, a thriving trade centre, there was a more subtle form of attack. Their livelihoods were under threat if they refused to compromise – and false teaching in the church was compounding their sense of confusion.

Thyatira was a busy marketplace. Apparently anyone who wanted to do business in the city was required to be a member of a 'trade guild'. These were numerous and at their heart was the worship of pagan gods and immoral celebrations. It is clear that the guilds played a strong part of the culture of citizenship.

How were the Christians to deal with this? They knew Paul had allowed Christians to eat meat bought in the market, although it had been killed for sacrifice to the gods. He said that association with idols that didn't exist could not contaminate them. But they should not eat meals in the temples because that would involve them in worshipping false gods. Some were not impressed by this, and thought that sexual immorality presented no problem either. Indeed, they vigorously defended it in the name of Christian freedom.

In Thyatira there was a self styled prophetess in the church who was encouraging the church to get fully involved in the guilds. The argument was persuasive – they were not under law anymore. They were being drawn into occult worship and immorality.

Faithfulness and loyalty are at the heart of Christ's call to these two churches. Jesus says that the way of conquest is by his word. He describes himself as he who has the sharp, double-edged sword. In the vision of the exalted Christ which John saw and described in Revelation 1 this sharp double-edged sword came out of his mouth (Rev.1:16) because it is a symbol of the word of truth which h has spoken. He is himself 'the Word of God' .

Faithfulness

Recognising the faithful
- Which members of the church have been committed members for a long time?
- What role do they play now?
- In what ways have they been faithful?

Faithfulness and personal honesty:

Our congregation is constantly changing – new people join and long standing members leave and change. Individuals are on a journey of faith, with its crises, joys, and struggles.

- How do we make space for that?
- What opportunity is there to question the Christian faith and be open and honest?
- Is this encouraged and if so how?
- What ways are people encouraged to find their own answers?

Faithful in doctrine

▶ What are the key statements of Christian doctrine that your particular church community views as central to its identity? Look at this across the generations. There will be different replies, depending on the person's age or how long they have been members of the church. Those joining a church for the first time place less importance on forming an allegiance to a particular tradition. Instead, they have a growing emphasis on what actually goes on at a particular church and what's on offer.

▶ What is it that makes the church theologically distinctive from others in the area?
▶ Has the church changed in its view of doctrine in any way over the last ten years?
▶ How would you judge this?
▶ Have some things become less important and others more?
▶ How does the church's doctrinal view affect the church in action?
▶ What are the main theological influences in your church – is there one strong voice or do you have a diversity of voices?

Depending on the church context there are close links between a church's view on tradition and on Christian doctrine.

▶ How does the church address the relationship between these areas and what are the strengths and the challenges?
▶ How do we create a tolerant church community AND remain faithful to the gospel?

Faithful in ethics and integrity

▶ What is the church's understanding and approach to the Christian quality of holiness?
▶ Is holiness something that is seen as attainable or almost unachievable?
▶ How would it be recognised?
▶ When the church speaks out about or deals with ethical situations is it seen by church members as acting fairly?
▶ What vocabulary is used when talking about right and wrong?
▶ What sort of image does the local church have? Is it seen as being judgemental or permissive?
▶ Where would a member of the church go if they were in trouble?
▶ Where would a member of the local community go if they were in trouble?
▶ Is the ethical framework that is at the fore of the church's work clear or confused?
▶ What sort of people are allowed in and permitted to do things?
▶ Are there access rituals to attain church membership or leadership status? e.g attend a course, be able to show a certain understanding?
▶ What effect does this have?

Doctrine expressed through worship

- How does our time together equip us for our time apart? Worship – training – praying – listening – fellowship.
- How would you describe the worship in the church?
- Does the worship unite or divide people?
- Do the people come to your church mainly for the worship?
- How has the worship changed in the last two, five or ten years?
- What have been the key influences in this?
- What are the challenges facing the worship life of the church?
- What are the strengths of the worship in the church?
- Who is responsible for putting the services together?
- Are there others with gifts in leading or contributing to the worship of the church who are not being used or who need to take more responsibility?
- How does the worship life of the church reach the diverse needs of the church community?
- What are the challenges that are coming up?

> **Information Point**
> *Living Liturgy* Michael Perham
> *Using Common Worship Series*, Praxis/CHP, e.g. Using Common Worship: Holy Communion by Mark Beach
> *Emmaus*: Your kingdom Come

Discipline

- Does this have any role in your church?
- Is it there but called something else?
- Has it an active and crucial role?
- Does it provide security or not?
- If so, is this helpful or not?
- How does a loving and disciplined church work in reality?
- How can discipline and unconditional love work together?

Living with leadership

For the congregation and the leadership:
- What is a healthy view of leadership? Does your church have it?
- To whom are you accountable?
- Have you given anyone the right to speak into your life? Do you listen if they are critical?

- What do you do if you feel you are failing?
- What do you do if you are not coping – or members of your family?
- How do you cope with criticism?
- What do you do in the face of growing opposition?
- Who do you have that you can trust?
- Do you have a view of your weaknesses as well as your strengths?
- What would make you happy?
- What in the church makes you angry?
- How do you deal with your anger?
- What are the circumstances that make you frustrated?
- How does the work that you do affect your relationships with your partner and/or children?
- What adjustments in your work pattern have you made in the last year – or do you fell that you must make in the future?

For the leadership only:
- How do you know when it's time to move on?
- If there is a staff team, how does shared leadership work out in practice and who carries ultimate responsibility?

Faithful to the prophetic

- Is prophecy a word that is used in your church?
- If it's used often is it useful?
- If it's not used at all what do people see prophecy as?
- How does the gift of prophecy contribute to church life in worship and mission?
- Is it happening but talked about using other language?
- What have been the long-term benefits of this gift?

Faithful to the gifts for the church

- What teaching is there on the gifts for the church?
- What gifts are well developed and widely accepted in the church?
- Which ones are the church more suspicious of or have a need for?

Women in leadership

▶ When was it in the life of the church that women took a lead role?
▶ Has the view of women in leadership changed in your church over the last ten years?
▶ How ?
▶ What is the next step?
▶ Who can be an effective help in this?
▶ Do you have a balanced staff team – does it suit the community you serve?
▶ How are people encouraged to follow their calling to lead or for ordination according to your tradition?
▶ Is there a gap in the team?
▶ Is there someone that you think could be encouraged to take the next step?

> **ℹ Information Point**
> *Introduction to Christian Ministry*: Gordon Kuhrt (CHP)

Our different needs

A loyal community
▶ What facilities are there on the church premises to cater for those with physical needs?
▶ How can the building be improved for people with different needs – e.g. wheelchair users, those with visual problems, hard of hearing, learning difficulties.
▶ How does this effect the things that happen in the church and activities that are part of the life of the church?
▶ How does the church cope with anyone who is seen as being different?
▶ How diverse is the church community?
▶ Does it represent the area that it is part of?
▶ If not, why and what can be done if this is important?

> **ℹ Information Point**
> *Through the Roof*, Global House, Ashley Avenue, Epsom, Surrey KT18 5AD.
>   t. 01372 749955   w. www.throughtheroof.org
>   f. 01372 737040   e. pdicken@throughtheroof.org
> *Widening the Eye of the Needle* (CHP)
> *Causeway PROSPECTS* is a mission to people with learning disabilities, providing resource materials and support for churches. Contact causeway@prospects.org.uk for information. For details of the residential work, contact info@prospects.org.uk; website www.prospects.org.uk

CHAPTER 5

The church as the long suffering community

Smyrna and Philadelphia were very different cities. Smyrna was a beautiful city that had been raised from the dead. Destroyed by an earthquake six hundred years before Christ, it was a desolate ruin for three hundred years. Rebuilt, it became a beautiful jewel of a place, known as the glory of Asia. It was still a deep water port, and its inhabitants enjoyed wide streets, the largest theatre in Asia Minor, and many temples to the Greek gods – Cybele, Zeus, Apollo, Asklepios, and Aphrodite. The whole city was a model of meticulous town planning, built around the fourth century BC and enjoying a flourishing wine trade. It was also famous for its science and medicine.

Sixty miles east of Smyrna lay the new city of Philadelphia. This city had originally been built as a mission outpost for Greek culture and civilisation and was the last bastion of Greek thinking before the wildness of the barbarians began. The city had been built with the intention of converting the Phrygian barbarians to the Greek way of thinking – but this had been unsuccessful. With the city's close proximity to an volcano, the soil was ideal for vines but there was the frequent danger of volcanic activity. People lived very unsettled lives, frequently having to flee and the population was constantly changing. The city was very pagan, and so many gods were worshipped that it became known as 'little Athens'. The principle god was Dionysius, the god of wine.

We don't know how the church in Smyrna was started. Polycarp, a disciple of the Apostle John was the leader of the church for many years. Like the apostle, he had no time for heretics. He had to confront Marcion, a wealthy ship owner who tried to cleanse Christianity of all that was Jewish. Polycarp's description of him was 'the first born of Satan.' Philadelphia was a small church, possibly a church plant from Smyrna or Colossae, Laodicea or Hierapolis.

There were very significant Jewish communities in both places and they were actively hostile to the Nazarenes – the Christians. Ultimately it was the Jewish voices, together with those of the pagans, that called for Polycarp's execution. The Christians were frequently subject to attacks on their property, imprisonment and death threats.

Of the seven churches that 'got mail' from Christ, only two of them received no words of criticism at all; Smyrna and Philadelphia. They were singled out only for words of encouragement and commendation. This was not because they were perfect but because they were steadfast through immense suffering.

The death of Smyrna's leader Polycarp was a powerful illustration of the passionate faith that fuelled the hearts of courageous believers. The elderly leader refused to compromise and paid the ultimate price for his faith.

Today, half the population of Smyrna is Christian; the city is one of the great centres of learning and worship of the Eastern Orthodox Church. Philadelphia is a Christian town with a Christian Bishop. It is still a town of considerable size, called *Allahshehr* 'the city of God'.

How the church helps those who suffer

- ▶ How does the church help, in big and little ways, those who suffer?
- ▶ What does the church offer in its services and worship life for those who want comfort and healing?
- ▶ Are any of these accessible for those who are not regular church members?
- ▶ Are there ways in which the church exercises a healing ministry?
- ▶ How does the church share a prayer ministry that is open to all and encourages active participation? This could range from lighting candles to a prayer board, a prayer chain, a welcoming church with unlocked doors, a simple said liturgy or healing services.

The extraordinary situation:
- ▶ How did your church react to the recent international crisis?
- ▶ What was the reaction of the local community?
- ▶ When has the church been a help to the community?

The church's role in the caring network of the wider community.
- ▶ Do you have connections with bereavement organisations or employment agencies or other support agencies, for the house-bound – for the retired – for the young families – for marriage – for relationships etc.
- ▶ What follow up is provided for those who recently had funerals of loved ones? Are there any groups run by the church or a visiting programme for the recently bereaved?

Long term projects, relationships in the community

- ▶ What jobs or positions at work and in the community do church members hold that can be built into a network of supportive relationships?

Health service links

▶ How can the church strengthen links with the local hospitals?
▶ Is there a role for your church in the local hospitals alongside a chaplaincy team?
▶ Who could fulfil this role?
▶ How could the church be used in the local nursing homes e.g. regular visiting programme or taking services, offering home communion, special services at Christmas or Easter etc?
▶ Health centres – does the church have a role to play here?

School links

Pre school provision – play groups and toddlers activity groups
▶ What is the present local provision for pre school-age children?
▶ What could the church provide for the community to complement what is already there?
▶ Are there possible partnerships that could be created for early years? This may involve play-groups, nurseries, school foundation stage staff and the church. This facilitates working together on specific projects and share training and resources.

Primary and secondary education:
▶ What is the history of the church's links with schools? This will take into account the school's status e.g. voluntary aided, voluntary controlled, county etc.
▶ If the church has links to any schools in the area, how can they be built up?
▶ What role does the church play in the school?
▶ How is this a part of the mission to the whole community?
▶ Where do you go to for support and contacts to work on these links?
▶ Who in the congregation can help with this?
▶ What are the present strengths?
▶ What are the present challenges?
▶ What is the church's input into schools at Christmas, Harvest or Easter? Is the church shipped in to do the 'traditional Christmas' or can it be used creatively to be the Christian presence?

> *i* **Information Point**
> Diocesan Boards
> Care for Education 0207 233 0455
> Development Matters (CHP)

Social service links

▶ What is the employment situation in your area?
▶ Have you been in contact with your local council to discover what other provision there is in the community?
▶ Does your church have the resources/necessary skills/personnel to offer this kind of service to the community in a sustained manner?
▶ Could your church offer more than advice i.e. job training or employment opportunities?

For more detailed information in terms of
▶ Research
▶ Strategy
▶ Business planning
▶ Funding

read Faithworks Unpacked: A Practical Manual to Equip Churches for Community Involvement.

Information Point
Pecan – 0207 358 9003
Oasis – Oasis Trust, 115 Southwark Bridge Road, London SE1 0AX
    0207 4509049
Prisons: A study in vulnerability: Peter Sedgwick (CHP)
Citizen Advice Bureaux
Housing associations

Youth links

▶ When was the last time a young person experienced life to the full in your congregation?
▶ A fifteen year old girl happens to wander in to your Sunday morning service. Coming from an entirely un-churched background, she has never been to church before except for the day of her Grandmother's funeral. She stays for twenty minutes of the service. What impressions of God and his people does she leave with?
▶ What do the young people of your congregation think about your church?
    a. Is it a place they go to?
    b. Something they suffer?
    c. A functional family they feel part of?
    d. A mission they live for?

- How many young people have positions of responsibility within your day-to-day church life?
- Young people are desperate to make their lives count for something. They more than anyone know that life has to be bigger than the size of their stereo. What opportunities does your church provide for young people to be involved in changing the world?
- Which of these areas of live are made better for young people by them being part of your church community?
  a. Home life
  b. School work
  c. Career prospects
  d. Holidays
  e. Friendship groups
  f. Skills, gifts and interests
- How has your churched help young people to understand their own world and culture?
- One expert has said that much youth work in the new millennium will take the shape of 're-parenting' young people. How can your church provide young people with deep and meaningful relationships with adults.
- How can your church provide a safe place for young people to be honest about their struggles?
- Where would your present young people go with questions about drugs and addictions, sexuality and sexual orientation, abuse and self-harm:
  a. Peers
  b. School teacher
  c. Social worker
  d. Agony aunt
  e. Internet chat room
  f. Church member
  g. Minister
  h. Parent / family member
- What would you like the age profile of your church to look like in twenty years? How close will you be to this with your present rate of growth?
- What unnecessary persecution does the church bring upon itself by the way it fails to be incarnate in its community?
- Sometimes the church's behaviour brings it a totally justifiably bad press – but the church interprets this as persecution. As a church, do we fit our community and if not, is that more to do with any immovable attitudes we may have?
- Has the church made itself irrelevant to its community and how has this happened? What steps can the church take to be a new, seen and relevant presence in the community?

Looking to the future – new ways of being church

This book would not be complete without raising the challenge to the church of seeking new ways of being church. Michael Moynahan has written a book Changing world, Changing church. I do not see the need to stop all that we have been doing and be new for the sake of it, but if this book says anything, it says that we cannot be complacent. We cannot take it for granted that as a local church we will always exist.

- What are the possibilities for the future with what we have got?
- What new ways can we develop that continue to build a strong church in your community? What partnerships can be made?
- What teams of people can learn to work together?
- How can we be an open welcoming church who can be a message of good news to those we live with?

This is not free licence to start a church in competition to other churches but more the need for churches to assess themselves and be aware of the responsibility they have to grab the moment and ask the questions.

i Information Point
Changing world, changing church Michael Moynagh – Monarch books 2001

Come Lord Jesus

The church, which has been long suffering is finding ways of rising from its state of inertia and facing the present struggle. We are waiting as the Bride of Christ to emerge from the shadows and begin to stand with stature, not because it is our right but because it is our desire. We want to see the church be useful to those who do not see their need for it: vital to those who had dismissed it, loved by those who had been suspicious of it, and to rise from the ashes of all that can hold us back.

CHAPTER 6

What next?

How are you going to translate all this into action? Are you going to keep it theoretical – just thoughts in your head or as interesting discussion points with your friends, or are you going to try to tackle all the issues, all at once?

Be selective – choose one area:
▶ Who are the people you want to involve?
▶ Who are the people you need to involve?
▶ How do you communicate?
▶ What obstacles need to be overcome?
▶ What opportunities are there?
▶ What tools have you got?

First
▶ So where are we now?
▶ What are we good at?
▶ Who do we have?
▶ Where have we come from in the last five years – in the last two years? – or in the last year?
▶ Encouragements – list them
▶ Challenges – list them

Second
▶ What is our next focus?
▶ Have we one within the church community and within the wider community?
▶ How does the focus relate to our strengths and weaknesses?

Third
▶ What is our long term vision?
▶ Can we really dream our dreams in a session – as a leader, where would you want the church to be in one year – five years?

Churches do not leap from one step of action to another. This book is not meant to oversimplify the process by which a church's journey of faith in action emerges. But it is so easy to avoid asking the questions that will stimulate thinking and direct the way ahead.

The life of a community of faith is not determined by the type of song or hymn they sing and how well or how many times they sing it but by

▶ Being accessible to the community it belongs to.
▶ Being diverse in its character and composition and tolerant of one another.
▶ Having an awareness of its place in the community and what it offers and what it receives.

The challenge may be great but with courage, wisdom and faith together we will continue to travel on – getting there.